LONDON UNDERGROUND
in Colour
for the Modeller and Hist

John Glover

Ian Allan
PUBLISHING

Cover:
For the Northern Line station at
East Finchley, Eric Aumonier designed
'The Archer', pointing his arrow of vitality
and progress towards London. This station,
by Holden with L. H. Bucknell, first saw
Underground trains arrive via the extension
from the present Archway on 3 July 1939.
Services ran on to High Barnet on 14 April
1940. The LNER steam services from
Finsbury Park ceased on 2 March 1941,
never to be resumed in any form, though
freight continued for another 20-odd years.
The spiral staircase in the rounded end of the
station building seen here on 29 June 2008
leads to staff accommodation above.

Title page:
The overall roof at the Metropolitan's
Notting Hill Gate station is the most
complete one still in existence, and is seen
here looking north towards Paddington
on 9 March 2008. The elegant wrought-iron,
arch-rib roof spans the gap between the walls,
and it gives a light and airy (or sometimes
perhaps draughty) feeling to the platforms.
The station was opened on 1 October 1868,
but was not linked directly to the Central Line
station until 1959.

All photographs by the Author

First published 2009

ISBN 978 0 7110 3349 8

© Ian Allan Publishing Ltd 2009

Published by Ian Allan Publishing

An imprint of Ian Allan Publishing Ltd, Riverdene
Business Park, Molesey Road, Hersham, Surrey
KT12 4RG

Code: 0906/B1

Visit the Ian Allan Publishing website at:
www.ianallanpublishing.com

INTRODUCTION

The passenger station is an integral part of a railway system. It is primarily the place where passengers can board and alight from trains in safety, and where in general terms the passenger meets the service provider, and makes the commercial transaction of purchasing a ticket. There are, of course, more features to a station than just that, but in essence its role as a passenger terminal is its most significant.

However, in the early days of the railway, the station had more aesthetic purposes. During that time there was a need to impress the passenger, and the railway wanted to portray an image of a fine upstanding company which spared no expense and would take good care of its clients' needs. First impressions counted, and the railway companies hoped that their passengers would not only enjoy a relaxing journey, but also recognise the craft that had gone into the intricate designs of the stations.

This book examines the way in which the stations, served by what is now London Underground, have evolved and developed from the earliest days to the present time. There is a distinct series of phases, in which differing concerns and objectives were the responsibilities of a succession of businessmen, managers and politicians.

The term 'station' refers to the entrances, ticket halls, access routes, platforms and associated buildings – or their below-ground equivalents. It does not normally include the permanent way, signalling or any electrification plant.

THE SYSTEM

The first underground line in London was that of the Metropolitan Railway, whose 1863 line ran from Paddington to Farringdon Street (not the present Farringdon). This line, its extensions and its competitors, were all built by the cut-and-cover method, or at least where they were traversing areas of London which were already built up. The method was to cut a deep trench, ideally the width of two tracks, build the railway in the trench, and then cover it over. This would most usually mean the reinstatement of a road, or perhaps the construction of commercial premises.

The lines so built were, besides today's Metropolitan Line, the District (originally the Metropolitan District but an entirely separate company), and what are today known as the Circle and the Hammersmith & City Lines. Traction was by steam locomotive, the stations were a staircase or two below street level, and there was much in common with the ordinary railway which by now was penetrating most of Britain. The adequacy of ventilation was a particular problem, and even in Victorian London these lines did not rate highly on what would now be called environmental grounds. Collectively, these are referred to as the subsurface lines of the Underground.

The second stage was the introduction of the deep-level bored tunnel, the means of construction coining the word 'tube', by which the whole system is now generally known. The first such line was the City & South London Railway, from King William Street (near Monument) to Stockwell; it was the first section of which, over the next half-century, was to become today's Northern Line. It opened in 1890.

For the tube railway to become a reality, four technical problems had to be solved. First was the tunnelling, carried out by the advancement of an underground shield, with the tunnels lined with cast-iron segments as it progressed. Second was the ventilation, which was helped by the piston effect of the trains fitting the tunnels tightly, albeit often at the expense of draughts along the platforms. On its own, this was found insufficient, and ventilation shafts were constructed. Third was the means of traction; electricity was the only practicable means, but electric traction had to be brought to a satisfactory state of development. Last was passenger access to a relatively deep level, for which the lift was the chosen method. This too needed to be developed, especially with regard to passenger safety. Escalators, though in many ways superior to lifts as long as the depths were not too great, were still the best part of 20 years away.

Throughout the central area, tube lines were built at a remarkable rate, and the subsequent and inevitable financial problems of such were resolved when the American financier, Charles Tyson Yerkes, pledged his support. That some of the tube lines were ever built at all is probably the result of Yerkes's intervention, however questionable his financial practices. The tube lines thus established were still limited to the then built-up-area, and were therefore almost entirely underground. An early exception was the Bakerloo Line, which ran over the tracks of the London & North Western Railway, giving access to Watford Junction by 1917. This period also saw the electrification of most of the subsurface networks.

The net result was that all the Underground lines in the present day Fare Zone 1 had been built by the outbreak of World War 1 in 1914. This left only the much later Victoria Line (1968-71) and the Jubilee Line (1979 and 1999) to complete the present central area network.

Organisationally, Underground Electric Railways of London (UERL) was formed in

1902 and gradually acquired all the subsurface and tube railways then in existence, apart from those of the Metropolitan Railway. That company staunchly maintained its independence until it was subsumed into the newly formed London Passenger Transport Board in 1933. Apart from the outskirts of the Metropolitan, almost everything was by then electrified.

The Waterloo & City Line remained part of what was later British Rail, until it too became part of London Underground in 1994.

BEYOND
CENTRAL LONDON

While the tube railways were finding their feet, the Metropolitan and the District expanded quickly, to the extent that virtually the whole of the present subsurface network was in place by 1914. It was the tube lines which had much further to go, and by 1939 they had reached Ealing Broadway (1920), Edgware (1924), Morden (1926), Cockfosters (1933), and Uxbridge (1938). Metropolitan trains got to Stanmore in 1932, to be replaced by tube services in 1939.

But that was not all. Other extensions were designed to take over some of the tracks of the Great Northern, Great Eastern and Great Western Railways. There was a dual aim of

Above: This platform level-view of **Great Portland Street** shows the eastbound platform from the westbound on 7 May 2008. Although constructed originally for the 7ft 0¾in broad gauge, opportunity was later taken to extend the platforms outwards, though they are still not over-wide.
The brightening up of the walls by the use of buff or similar-coloured paints helps to relieve the rather gloomy effect, but what conditions must have been like in the days of steam traction is perhaps best left to the imagination.

Below: The exterior of the highly unusual **Kennington** station is the dividing point for the City and West End branches of the Northern Line, but it is the only station of the former City & South London Railway to retain its surface building more or less intact. Designed by the company's architect Thomas Phillips Figgis (1858-1948), it features a red brick single storey building, surmounted by a lead dome for the lift mechanisms and with a cupola on the top of that. The station was opened on 18 December 1890; this view dates from 7 May 2008.

Right: **Mile End** is where the Central line extension from Liverpool Street rises each side of the District Line and affords cross-platform interchange between the two in both directions. This below-ground station thus has a very important function as well as serving the local area. Central Line services were inaugurated on 4 December 1946, but the original station was opened in 1902. This is a view of the outside of one of Holden's works, which seems to have an affinity with the Morden extension works rather than the more recent. This view of 29 March 2008 shows the continuing and now rare use of a roundel bearing the name 'London Transport'.

relieving these railways of relatively short-distance traffic which was causing severe system congestion, and providing a new standard of service to the areas concerned.

This, the New Works Programme 1935-40, saw the Northern Line reach beyond Archway to High Barnet (1940) and Mill Hill East (1941), but the combination of hostilities in the short term and post-war Green Belt legislation meant that no further progress would be made. The Central Line expansion programme was, however, resumed, and completed to Epping (1946-49) and West Ruislip (1947-48).

Steam passenger services were eliminated with the introduction of electric services to Amersham and Chesham (1960), when services beyond Amersham became the sole responsibility of British Railways. The Great Northern & City (Finsbury Park – Moorgate) followed suit in 1975. The Victoria Line (1968-72) and the Jubilee Line extensions which reached Stratford in 1999 were both notable in that the new services did not extend beyond Fare Zone 3. Very long journeys by Underground do have their shortcomings from the passenger's point of view.

In three separate stages, the Piccadilly Line was extended to a growing Heathrow.

THE STATIONS

This brief resumé of how the system developed is perhaps a necessary background to how the stations themselves were built. These were private companies, and building new railways of which a large portion would be below ground level was bound to be costly. At the same time, the extent to which the public would take to them (or not, as the case might be) was, at best, uncertain. Thus these were quite high-risk investments.

Among the results was that station (and other) facilities were kept to a reasonable minimum to avoid undue cost, and this manifested itself in a number of ways. Perhaps the most difficult in terms of its effect on subsequent generations was the decision to limit the physical diameter of the tube tunnels to a nominal 12ft or thereabouts, and even tighter on the City & South London (CS&LR). Smaller diameters mean that much less spoil can be removed – a considerable economy in tunnelling costs.

But while the CS&LR was closed for up to two years as part of the 1920s upgrading and linking it with tunnel enlargement to the Charing Cross, Euston & Hampstead, there have been no other examples of this. Other problems in many locations were platform lengths and widths being inadequate for the traffic on offer, and the need for escalators to replace (or occasionally supplement) lifts.

In short, the system generally did not have the capacity to deal with the growing levels of traffic, and this meant that large-scale investment was necessary. This was required not only to cope with higher passenger volumes, but also to right some of the unfortunate problems which had arisen from many lines being promoted privately by a number of different companies. Too little thought had been given to the needs of passengers to change between lines as part of their journeys.

Below: **Embankment** Northern Line northbound platform is seen on 21 May 2008. The original Charing Cross, Euston and Hampstead Railway used a terminal loop. Necessarily, this was of tight radius to minimise both tunnelling costs and land-take. When the large-scale rebuilding and amalgamation with the City & South London Railway took place in 1926, the line was extended to Kennington. A new straight southbound platform was constructed, but the northbound line used part of the original tunnel, which accounts for its severe curvature. This has the inevitable result of rather larger than desirable gaps between the centre doors of an Underground car and the platform edge.

PHASES OF DEVELOPMENT

1863 to 1918

This period saw the establishment of the cut-and-cover subsurface lines, more or less to full sized railway loading gauge. Many of the original buildings have been replaced over the years, often with enlargement as the principal aim.

The era also saw a similar development with the early tube lines, and the contribution of Leslie Green (1875-1908), whose 'ox-blood' tile design on his distinctive surface buildings and tiled platform walls incorporating the station name are instantly recognisable. Green was architect to UERL from 1903 and had over 50 stations to his credit in what turned out to be a tragically short life.

1919 to 1947

The expanding Metropolitan Railway had Charles Walter Clark (1885-1972) as its architect, whose major contribution was the rebuilding of many of the company's stations in a classical style to cater for traffic growth. His appointment ended with the creation of the London Passenger Transport Board in 1933.

For the Underground group, the period following World War 1 was one initially of consolidation, but it would soon herald further system expansion. It was during this period that the Underground's Frank Pick (1878-1941) spotted the latent talents of the architect Charles Holden (1875-1960). Pick, who rose to become Vice Chairman and Chief Executive of the Board, saw the fast-expanding transport system as a work of art, for which he wanted a new architectural idiom, and Holden (from the practice of Adams, Holden & Pearson) was the man to achieve it. The choice was well rewarded; both Pick and Holden had remarkably similar aims which were driven by the ideal of service. Thus Holden wrote in his later years: 'I want an architecture which is through and through good building. A building planned for its specific purpose, constructed in the method and use of materials, old or new, most appropriate to the purpose the building has to serve.' (1957).

Readers will be able to judge the results for themselves; in the opinion of Holden's biographer Eitan Karol 'The Underground was emblematic of modernism in Britain in the 1930s, and Holden defined a modern British architecture.'

Thus Holden gave an altogether new and exciting expression as to what an Underground station could be for the business, the passengers and the staff alike. He was responsible for the design of 57 stations. Between them, these two men transformed the appearance of an expanding Underground, for which it achieved worldwide recognition.

In 1937, the peak year before the war, 527 million journeys were made on the system. In 1948 the Board was nationalised as the London Transport Executive and became part of the British Transport Commission.

1948-1972

These were quiet years for the Underground, and there was little public money available in post-war Britain for anything other than the bare essentials and completing or abandoning work on business unfinished as a result of the onset of the war. The motor car was seen as the future, and Underground traffic levels stabilised at an annual total of around 650 million. New works were minimal; the government finally gave the long-talked-about Victoria Line the construction go-ahead in 1963, but perhaps as much to relieve unemployment as for its

Below: The Piccadilly Line station at **Wood Green**, opened 19 September 1932, is in the right place, just as that built in 1859 by the Great Northern Railway (now Alexandra Palace) is not. As can be seen, this is a busy location in the middle of the shopping area, and the relative patronage justifies such a conclusion. This is a Charles Holden station with a wide curved frontage, though with rather less window space than some other offerings. It is seen here on 23 June 2003.

Bottom: The two platforms at **Hounslow West** form an island and this is the view looking west towards Heathrow. They were opened on 19 July 1975, when the Piccadilly was extended in a first stage to Hatton Cross. The building method was cut-and-cover and the result is more reminiscent of subsurface operation, though the provision of a 'canopy' avoids the dark areas which usually accompany this type of station.

well-argued benefits to London. Only two stations, Blackhorse Road and Brixton produced new surface buildings.

1973-1999

Passenger volumes fell to 498 million in 1982, but recovered, at first slowly, then faster from the mid-1990s. They had reached 927 million by the end of the century. Investment remained at a low level, but London was changing notably with the development of Docklands and the extension of the Jubilee Line to serve the area. On the second extension from Green Park to Stratford, a new approach became apparent, with a wish to 'get away from the Holden stereotypes'. New ideas were encouraged, exemplified by the widely varying treatment of the new stations on the line.

Heathrow at long last became served by Underground, with the Piccadilly Line being extended successively to Terminals 1, 2, 3 (1975) and T4 (1986).

from 2000

Recent times have been dominated by the Private Public Partnership deals in which 30-year contracts with outside companies Tube Lines (BCV), Metronet (JNP) and Metronet (SSL) undertaking infrastructure renewal, including stations, on a large scale. The Metronet companies went into PPP Administration in 2006, to become directly owned by Transport for London in 2008. One of the major tasks was updating and rebuilding the infrastructure, stations included.

Passenger journeys topped one billion for the first time in 2005/06, and Heathrow T5 was served from its opening in 2008. The same year saw the opening of a new station at Wood Lane (Hammersmith & City Line).

Separately from its own operations, the Underground has also run over some of the lines of what are now known as National Railways. The reverse is also true, but to a lesser extent. There have also been transfers of line and station ownership at different periods; consequently the operators at stations where Underground trains call might not necessarily be London Underground operators. Such examples include Barking, Richmond and Wimbledon. Further changes took place with the creation of London Overground in late 2007. Willesden Junction, for instance, is now operated by London Overground, though those each side, Harlesden and Kensal Green, have become part of LU.

Thus the number of passengers carried on the Underground is now over double what it was in the low year of 1982, a quarter of a century ago.

The six busiest stations each see between 50 million and 75 million passengers a year, counting both those joining and alighting, but not those interchanging within the premises. In descending order, these six comprise Victoria, Waterloo, Oxford Circus, Liverpool Street, King's Cross St Pancras and London Bridge.

The system has grown a little, as discussed, but essentially a lot more people are being carried using much the same assets. This places greater strains on staff, trains and infrastructure alike, since there are severe and expensive difficulties in achieving large expansions of service levels.

UNDERGROUND STATION NEEDS

There are a number of different areas of a station, each of which requires separate consideration. These are:
The station entrance
The ticket hall
Access and interchange
Concourse(s) and platforms
Track requirements within the station area.

There are separate parameters for the capacity and arrangement of each, and in general terms there are three different types of stations. These are:
Surface stations
Sub-surface stations
Deep-level tube stations

A single site may contain more than one type; for instance, Westminster where the subsurface platforms for the Circle and District Lines lie above the deep-level Jubilee Line platforms, but all within the confines of one station. Both subsurface and deep-level tube stations are defined as 'underground' stations for the purposes of the Fire Precautions Act, 1971.

Some of the biggest problems in stations, and not only Underground ones, are the avoidance of congestion and the resilience to demand surge. The latter may stem from any number of causes, including crowd-attracting

events such as football matches, but also train-service disruption. There must also be adequate capacity for evacuation, should circumstances so dictate.

GOOD PLANNING

It is perhaps axiomatic that stations should be planned in such a way that promotes the free flow of passengers, while also giving them reasonable comfort in the waiting areas and engendering a sense of security.

One of the aims is to keep walking distances down to an achievable minimum, and cross-platform or at least same-level interchanges are a good way of doing this. Compare, for instance, the arrangements at Oxford Circus, where the change between the Bakerloo and Victoria lines is painless to the extent that this is the recommended route between Waterloo and King's Cross St Pancras, with that between either of these and the Central Line. In contrast, this is a long boring walk, with plenty of steps to negotiate as well.

What can be achieved with interchanges between lines depends on the physical layout. Thus the Northern and Central Lines meet at Tottenham Court Road more or less at right angles, but do not overlap. The eastern end of the Central Line platforms is close to the northern end of the Northern Line platforms, albeit of course at a different level. But this in turn either means congested platform-to-platform routes with much passenger activity concentrated in the nearest platform areas, or a much longer walk between the centres of each platform on a totally different route.

In a much newer installation, it can be a very long walk (and use of three escalators or sets of stairs) between the Jubilee and District/Hammersmith & City Lines at West Ham, but this too is dictated by physical constraints.

Left: 'Holes in the wall' nowadays usually refer to cash machines, but it is an accurate enough description of this, the more attractive of the two entrances to **Parsons Green** station, opened on 1 March 1880.
The platforms above are reached by stairs. Visiting many London Underground stations in the course of preparation of this book, the author was struck by the modest facilities offered by so many of them. It is 9 March 2008.

Right: The Underground is in debt to Edward Johnston, whose directional signage seen here at **Sudbury Town** performs the same task today as it has always done. It is simple, effective and easily understood. This view was taken on 22 March 2003.

PASSAGEWAYS

Walking routes in stations also need to be kept clear of obstructions, both so that users can anticipate and avoid collisions with those coming in the opposite direction, but also so that staff can get a good idea of what is happening. The route from the south end of the northbound Northern Line at Leicester Square to the westbound Piccadilly is decidedly tortuous in nature, though it is the most direct. The use of mirrors at the corners is helpful, but only a palliative.

It is also desirable to keep passageway flows to one direction wherever possible, though this is often not achievable. About the only way of enforcing this is to include a single escalator somewhere in the passage, which will certainly discourage travel in the wrong direction! More generally, cross-flows of passengers should be designed out as far as possible, though this depends on the respective volumes which might be encountered. Thus a single set of

Above: **Kennington** platforms on the Northern Line are laid out so that passengers have the benefit of same-level interchanges between trains for the Charing Cross and Bank branches, or as here between terminating trains and those continuing to Morden. Here, the southbound Charing Cross platform no 2 is typical of all other side platforms in tunnel on the Morden extension. That extends to the colour scheme: there are no variations. Of note are the large roundels bearing the station's name, which alternate between high and low level along the length of the platform. It is 21 May 2008.

escalators from the street, serving two lines such as at Holborn, will inevitably result in cross-movements at the bottom landing. Here, those entering the system turn left or right according to the line wanted, and meet those leaving the station and coming from right or left. There are also those staying within the station and merely changing lines.

WALKING SPEEDS

Passengers walk at varying speeds, but staircases inevitably slow everyone's pace. This means that such areas should be, if anything, slightly wider than the passageways they feed, if an even flow is to be maintained. A secondary consideration is when stairs need to be provided, or whether or not slopes are deemed sufficient. The odd single step in an otherwise unencumbered passageway is clearly not a good idea, and in general a staircase should consist of a minimum of three risers.

The peak-hour crowds also tend to move faster than those in the off-peak, partly because a high proportion of passengers know exactly where they are going and don't need to stop to check directions. However, passenger volumes do vary, and the peak hour itself is much busier than the three-hour period which together is usually designated as the peak. Similarly, the busiest 15-minute period is more than a quarter of the top hourly flow, and account has to be taken of the layout of the location concerned.

Thus the problem of the concourse areas, where the station operator has no wish to see large numbers of people halt to consider where they should go next. That points to such areas being of adequate size, but also emphasises the importance of clear and comprehensive signing. The limitations here can be to find sufficient space to hang the signs required, with a large enough typeface to be read easily and quickly. However, too many may lead to confusion. While tourism bodies may call for multi-lingual signs, where are they all going to be put?

TICKET HALLS

These are areas of multiple activities: besides the purchase of tickets from either a ticket window or a machine, they need to include a line of Underground Ticketing System gates, arrangements for excess-fare payments, information about fares, routes and train services, and adequate queuing and circulation spaces. This all needs to take into account the numbers involved in each activity, the likely pattern of movements, how long each activity will take the individuals concerned, and how the whole will change at different time periods.

Also needed is space for staff and station-related activities, and for any kiosks and public telephones. Increasingly, there are likely to be lifts for the mobility-impaired.

It is also highly desirable that the space available should not give rise to a feeling of claustrophobia, and this imposes minimum desirable dimensions of ceiling heights in particular. It is also helpful to provide for future expansion; thus although two escalators might be installed initially, the availability of space in the shaft to replace fixed stairs and install a third at some future date is desirable.

Another ticket hall-related issue is the distance between UTS gates and any escalator. Particularly for those finishing their journeys, there needs to be adequate space beyond the top of the escalator to absorb temporary congestion. More passengers being deposited by escalators into an area confined by ticket gates needs careful observation. That is one of the principal reasons for staffing the gates, so that they can be opened quickly and unconditionally.

PLATFORMS

Generally, platform dimensions determine the speed at which a platform clears after large numbers have alighted, aided or otherwise by the number of ways off the platform, and their purpose (for interchange, exit or both). Similar problems arise for those arriving on the platform and the conflict with those alighting. The train can only absorb the passengers who are waiting, so if those numbers are limited by congestion in the access-ways, the space on the train may not be as well utilised as it might be.

A further limitation is passengers departing where the same line serves more than one branch. Circle Line passengers at St James's Park may have to wait for a succession of Wimbledon, Richmond and Ealing Broadway services to appear before a Circle Line train. These passengers also occupy platform space.

Particularly with newer installations, platforms are as straight as can be achieved. Platform curvature in the horizontal plane limits the ability of staff and passengers alike to see along its length, and can produce uncomfortably large gaps between the platform and the train. A common cause was the desire to tunnel below the streets rather than the adjacent properties, with the risk of claims for subsidence or similar.

There are no easy solutions short of constructing a new alignment, which would be extremely disruptive as well as very costly.

Platform width is also a limitation, and the desire to pare down the Victoria Line construction costs wherever possible can be seen in their relatively substandard widths. Not all platforms are of the same width throughout their lengths, being less at the ends and greater in the middle. This can be observed at Oxford Circus on the Bakerloo Line, for instance.

Below: The 1935-40 New Works Plan envisaged the use of some nine-car trains on the Northern Line, despite the obvious problems that this would bring at stations with shorter platforms. In the event, the brand new **Highgate,** which opened on 19 January 1941, was the only one with longer platforms. This view is of the northbound on 29 June 2008, and the vastness of the space thus created is notable. At least it provided additional air-raid shelter space 'for the duration'.

Above: For a tube station, **Arsenal** is unusual in that there are no lifts or escalators, only long passageways and stairs. Because of the crowds on occasion, a secondary route has been created (in the cage on the left) to allow passengers to enter or leave the station when the main flow is in the opposite direction. At other times, this route is kept locked out of use. It is 10 April 2008.

STATION CONTROLS

Other requirements are the provision of a central station control point, normally in the ticket office area, equipped with CCTV and communications to staff and emergency services, with public address to reach passengers wherever on the premises they might be.

Potential hazards, and the means of overcoming them as well as can be devised, must also be identified and plans made accordingly. Any given station premises has its limitations, and the staff must know what they are, recognise if such conditions are developing, and take action as appropriate.

Overcrowding of platforms is one such event. This may be caused by shortcomings in train service operation, or perhaps the arrival of large numbers of fans at the end of a sporting event who all want to get away. The use of lattice gates within the premises which can be closed, barrier control, the use of public address or other ways of passing information to passengers and staff presence generally can all help.

If this is still not enough, the station itself may have to be closed to all new arrivals. This takes time and people to organise it as is deemed necessary. Even that may be only partially successful, since interchange stations provide an additional source of passengers from other lines. *In extremis* this can mean trains on those lines being sent through non-stop, but that is a job for Network Control to arrange.

There are also the more general issues of station security, crowd control, public order, queues, obstruction, and behavioural matters.

Similarly, what are the station staffing requirements, by areas of the station? To what extent should there be platform attendance for train despatch? After all, you never find staff at bus stops. There are particular requirements for stations which are deemed to be underground by the Fire Precautions Act, and these must be adhered to.

Other operational jobs at stations include cleaning and maintenance.

SYSTEMS

Much of the preceding discussion concerns stations which are truly underground, since almost by definition these are the most constrained and with little opportunity for change. However, the same principles apply elsewhere, with platform access always having to be made available. The island platform makes for economy of provision and staffing since only one waiting room is provided, but always requires steps or some form of assisted access.

Side platforms may have street access available directly from each side, but there has to be some means of crossing the tracks. Where the line is on a viaduct or in a cutting, footbridges or steps/subways are needed, again preferably with access for the mobility-impaired. Much progress continues to be made in the provision of fully accessible stations.

Another element in terms of train operation is the relationship of each station to others on the line. Thus if most of the platform entry points on a particular line are mainly at the western end at busy times, that part of the train will become uncomfortably full, with other parts relatively empty. 'Pass along the platform please' is not much heard nowadays, but such requests still have a purpose.

BUSY AND LESS BUSY

Also to be accommodated is the fact that some stations are far busier than others, even if they are quite nearby each other. Thus few would doubt which of the Piccadilly Line succession of Russell Square, King's Cross St Pancras and Caledonian Road is the busiest. That means longer station dwell times, though this is more a train operation problem than that of the stations themselves. Much here will depend on how the service is planned and specified.

Even so, the arrival of a train of Eurostar passengers at St Pancras International will bring in many Underground passengers who are unfamiliar with both the system and the language, and who probably have quite a bit of luggage. Such passengers will make disproportionate demands on station facilities, though this is an event which only happens at quite extended intervals.

PUBLIC APPRECIATION

Buildings used by the public in huge numbers will invariably be commented on, in terms of how good or otherwise they are to use and their ability to do the task for which they were designed, and so on. But, in another sense, how are they perceived by the public? This is something about which both users and non-users will express their opinion.

A station can and perhaps should be a subject of municipal pride, representing as it does an access point for the locality. The architecture might be seen as lasting, notable, mediocre, uncared for, or of no merit whatsoever.

This book does not attempt to chart the fashions of the times and how they change – as they inevitably will. Readers can assess this for themselves from the illustrations. However, it is perhaps worth mentioning that new ideas and new approaches are not always welcomed. Thus the extensive station works of Charles Holden may be generally appreciated today, but it was not always so.

Similarly, the tiling and the general approach to tube station facades developed by Leslie Green were sometimes less than admired. The following was the view of Christian Barman, himself an architect, who worked as publicity officer for London Transport during the later Holden period. This opinion was published in 1979:

The designers of the old Underground stations in central London had developed a type of station front made up of a row of big arches which could either be left open or filled in with walling. The station as a rule occupies a site with a long street frontage; there are seldom fewer than four arches and

Below: The southbound platform at **Angel** is still used for its former purpose and this is the view looking south along it on 28 May 2008. While it may strike today's passenger as generously proportioned as indeed it is, it now seems remarkable that a second track could have been fitted in next to the right-hand wall. But so it was for nearly a century, and this arrangement can still be seen at Clapham North and Clapham Common.

sometimes up to ten. The arches are tall enough to contain a low upper storey providing space for the lift machinery. Their architecture today seems singularly unattractive, they are pompous in manner; their colour, the colour of ox liver – about the most unattractive ever used in the streets of London – looked almost black when lit up by the street lights at night.

Perhaps on a less contentious note, it might be agreed that a well-presented and well-sited station will maximise the catchment area and the attractiveness of the railway system serving it. That must be to the gain of the local communities. Put another way, if it is in the right place and doing a good job, everybody will benefit.

Thus there is every reason to build stations as long term assets for the area, of which the population can be proud.

CONCLUSION

Finally, it might be noted that the scenes depicted in this book are there today for anybody to visit and enjoy, for the price of an Underground fare. The aim has been to provide a cross-section of the various architectural styles and approaches used over the life of London Underground, with a little bit of the history of how and why they were brought into being as they were. Some of these stations have now been around for the best part of a century and a half, and there is much, much more to be seen.

If this book whets the appetite of the reader sufficiently to encourage further exploration of the system, the author will be well satisfied.

John Glover
July 2008

Right: **Mornington Crescent** (1908) is one of the lesser-used stations on London Underground; when its original and ageing lifts needed replacing in 1992 the station was closed, and this might have turned out to be permanent. Funding was found though, and it reopened in 1998. The opportunity was taken to give this Leslie Green station a good clean up, and this was the result as seen on 27 September 1999. It is a relatively shallow station, with only 46 steps on the emergency stairs.

Right: The Victoria Line was finished throughout in greys, which later were seen as decidedly gloomy. This included the **Brixton** terminus, opened on 23 July 1971, which required a direct exit to the street from this totally underground line. It was one of the few stations not to have a direct interchange with another Underground or National Rail line. The entrance was rebuilt for the 21st century, resulting in this eye-catching display as seen on 22 April 2008. This can hardly be missed by those using Brixton Road.

Left: Opened on 23 December 1865 as Aldersgate Street, but becoming **Barbican** in 1968 after several renamings, this city station has two platforms (left) for the Underground and two for the Widened Lines. These latter ceased to be used between Farringdon and Moorgate from spring 2009 as a result of Thameslink works. The minimal facilities result in part from wartime bombing, the overall roof being dismantled and replaced by shelters. The roof supports can still be seen in this view looking east on 7 May 2008.

Below: The joint venture with the Great Western Railway beyond Paddington was opened to Hammersmith on 13 June 1864, though the present **Westbourne Park** Hammersmith & City station dates from 1 November 1871. Other platforms served the main line, but services were withdrawn and that part of the station closed on 16 March 1992, after which it became the responsibility of London Underground. This picture shows part of the very lengthy street frontage of the station on 9 April 2008, in typical GWR style. It is on a bridge over the railway. The four signs protruding from the brickwork all read: 'This queue is for the Underground only'.

Right: This view of the eastbound platform at **Westbourne Park** on 9 March 2008 shows how railings can act not only as separators between flows of people, but also to keep passengers clear of the tracks. It also encourages them to move along the platform rather than congregate at one end. The valances on the canopies have been retained here and at many other Underground stations; the problems of the clearances associated with overhead electrification do not exist.

Below: The frontage of **Hammersmith H&C** station is seen here on 5 June 2008, and again a strong Great Western style is apparent. Inside is a concourse with ticket office, together with a small arcade of shops, plus one side and one island platform. All are at street level. This station was opened on 1 December 1868, but was reconstructed to the present style in 1907-9 to a design by P E. Cumberhouse.

Left: The **Bayswater** station frontage, seen here on 26 April 2008, is an original building with some alterations since it was opened on 1 October 1868. It was designed by Sir John Fowler, the Metropolitan's engineer. The building stands on a road bridge at right angles over the tracks, which were built in a cutting with brick retaining walls.

Below left: The one part of the **Bayswater** station platform area which is not truly underground is the stairways descending from the entrance to the platforms. These are seen here on 28 June 2008. The stairs form a symmetrical arrangement around the entrance, and this short portion of the overall roof survives. The view looks north towards Paddington.

Above right: On the south side of the Circle Line, the Metropolitan and District Railways came together at **Gloucester Road** station, the street level building of which is seen here on 11 March 2008. This too is an original station from the hand of Sir John Fowler, built by the Metropolitan and opened by them on 1 October 1868; there have been subsequent alterations. At track level below, the most northerly platform is no longer used and art exhibitions are mounted on it from time to time. They are protected by their position in that there is no public access.

Right: **Neasden** station retains some of its Metropolitan Railway character; it was opened on 2 August 1880 as Kingsbury & Neasden. In 1939 the main service provider changed from the Metropolitan to the Bakerloo Line for the next 40 years, then to the Jubilee Line in 1979. The centre part of the main building has been rebuilt, though the ends are original.

Left: The entrance to **South Kensington** is from stairs in the middle of an arcade of shops dating from 1907, itself one of the first to be constructed anywhere. It can be entered from either end; this is the Pelham Street entrance. Here, the surface station for the Piccadilly Line (no longer used) was erected and is just visible on the right hand side of this picture, which was taken on 11 March 2008. The original stations were opened for the Metropolitan on 24 December 1868, the District on 1 August 1870 and the Piccadilly on 8 January 1907.

Right: This rather fine example of wrought-iron work showing the owning companies of the Metropolitan and District Railways was photographed on 11 March 2008 above the entrance to **South Kensington** station. This was the work of George Sherrin, inspired by the Arts & Crafts movement of the time.

Below: The facilities now shared by the District and Circle Lines at **South Kensington** fit comfortably onto a centrally-located island platform, which is now the sole passenger accommodation on the subsurface lines here. Seen here on 11 March 2008 is a disused eastbound platform, served by one of the outer tracks of what was once a four-tracked formation. In a way it is wasted capacity, but nobody can think of anything worthwhile to do with it.

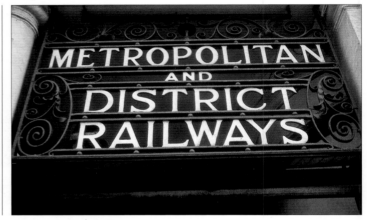

Left: The sub-surface **Sloane Square,** opened on 24 December 1868, has been an unfortunate station. Escalators were installed in 1940 as part of its rebuilding, with it all to be destroyed later that same year by World War ll bombing. Fortunately, the dark blue conduit seen here, in which the culverted River Westbourne crosses the station area, was not breached. The station was rebuilt yet again in 1951 and was one of the last to retain a licensed bar on the platform. This view looking east was taken on 11 March 2008.

Right: **Temple** station was opened on 30 May 1870 as one of the District Railway's stations built using the Victoria Embankment. The present building seen here on 22 April 2008 dates from 1911; it was designed by the District's architect, Harry Warton Ford (1875-1947). The intention was to blend the work with nearby Somerset House. The balustrade on the flat roof acts as a guard rail, a rather more elegant feature than the crude railings so commonplace today.

Left: The platforms at **Temple**, together with the supports with their leaf motifs, were pictured on 22 April 2008. The eastbound platform is seen from the westbound. The proximity of the yellow line to the platform edge will be noted, something which is achievable when all trains have sliding doors.

Left: The original **Earl's Court** station of 1871 was slightly further east, but was replaced in 1878. Reconstruction followed and this is the station entrance at the eastern end fronting onto Earl's Court Road, as it was on 9 March 2008. It was designed by Harry Warton Ford in conjunction with Leslie Green (see later) and was opened on 15 December 1906.

Below left: Train indicators of this antiquity (*c*1906) are quite a feature, though many passengers would probably prefer the more explanatory modern versions. Nevertheless they work, even if the next train only is shown. This display used to be on the eastbound island platform at **Earl's Court**, but was removed while the whole of this area underwent substantial refurbishment.

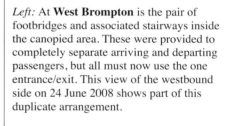

Above: From 12 April 1869, **West Brompton** was the terminus of the District Railway; continuation towards Putney Bridge was another 11 years away. The station is still much in its original form, and survives as a typical District product. Situated above the tracks, the entrance also now provides access to the new platforms on the West London Line, opened on 30 April 1999. That accounts for the recent tower on the right of this picture, photographed on 9 March 2008.

Left: At **West Brompton** is the pair of footbridges and associated stairways inside the canopied area. These were provided to completely separate arriving and departing passengers, but all must now use the one entrance/exit. This view of the westbound side on 24 June 2008 shows part of this duplicate arrangement.

Left: Seen from the eastbound platform at **West Brompton**, an Edgware Road-Wimbledon train of C stock arrives on 22 April 2008. The bridgeworks are under the 66ft long canopy shown in this picture; extensive cleaning and refurbishment of the wall on the right have added to the attractiveness of this station. It is also very near the Earl's Court exhibition hall as can be seen, and the station makes a good alternative access point for those attending events.

Left: **Fulham Broadway** station until recent years had a vast overall roof, but this has been shrunk to that which can be seen in this 9 April 2008 view looking south through the tunnel beneath Fulham Road and towards Putney Bridge. The present arrangements do at least afford much more direct pedestrian access to Chelsea Football Club's Stamford Bridge ground. The area of the station behind the photographer has been rafted over and incorporates all station facilities which were previously reached via the footbridge shown but which now leads nowhere.

Centre left: The exterior of Putney Bridge & Fulham station as it was known from its 1880 opening, later Putney Bridge and Hurlingham, before becoming plain **Putney Bridge** in 1932. Such names and that of the District Railway owners previously graced the conspicuously empty light-grey areas on the façade. This grand building seen here on 10 April 2008, with the trains on the viaduct behind it, has bus stops providing a number of services immediately outside. It is the station for Craven Cottage, Fulham FC's ground.

Below left: The present island at **Putney Bridge** serving Platforms 2 & 3 was built as a side platform (present no 2) and converted to its present state upon electrification in 1910. Unfortunately, No 2 which is a bay is only long enough to accommodate C stock trains, so the reversal of D stock can only be done via the sidings at Parsons Green or by continuing to Wimbledon. The platform number indicator seen here on 9 March 2008, complete with the pigeon netting, is the original.

Above right: The station entrance at **Southfields** seen here on 19 March 2005 and the very similar one at Wimbledon Park are both on the portion of line built and operated by the London & South Western Railway. This carried Underground trains from its opening on 3 June 1889; LSWR use did not start until a month later. The entrances of both have been described a 'red brick buildings with pyramid roofs and tall chimney stacks', which sums them up admirably. The company name and year of opening are featured above the entrance.

Right: **Wimbledon Park** station platforms are seen from the road bridge, looking south towards an arriving train of C stock on 19 March 2005. Although passenger services here by what was then the Southern Railway ceased in 1941, the line is used today by South West Trains for depot access and as a diversionary route as far north as East Putney. The line was transferred to London Underground in 1994.

Left: This is **North Ealing**, an original Metropolitan District Railway station which opened on 23 June 1903. The upper floor was used for living accommodation. Here, the platforms are in a cutting, and that for eastbound trains is reached via a footbridge which unusually starts from outside the building itself. The service from Acton Town to Rayners Lane and Uxbridge is today part of the Piccadilly Line, having been transferred from the District in 1932/3. It was photographed on 22 March 2003.

Right: This is a general view of **North Ealing** platforms looking south towards Acton Town on 22 March 2003. It is in many ways a simple and attractive wayside station which could have been built by one of the main-line companies. Today its use includes much in the way of schools traffic, adding a seething and cacophonous mass to this quiet location for short periods of time.

Left: This enamel sign 'To Trains For Harrow and Uxbridge' is a long term survivor at **North Ealing**, seen here on 22 March 2003. It greets passengers accessing the westbound platform. Those for Harrow will, of course, need to change at Rayners Lane.

Left: This is the frontage of the extensive and impressive **Barons Court** District and Piccadilly lines station, though only the District Company is acknowledged above the entrance. That company's trains arrived on 9 October 1905, with the Piccadilly just over a year later. The station is the work of Harry Warton Ford and was photographed on 29 June 2008.

Right: The ticket office area at **Barons Court** has retained its mottled green tiling and the elaborate ticket office windows, despite changes necessary as a result of the present ticketing system. It leads, via the ticket gates, to a footbridge from which steps descend to both island platforms. It is 9 April 2008.

Left: Station seating needs to be reasonably compact to fit the relatively tight space available, and these double-sided examples at **Barons Court** certainly comply. There are three on each island, their height making it possible to display a large enamel station sign for the benefit of passengers. This example seen on 10 April 2008 is on the westbound platforms, Piccadilly near side and District on the far side.

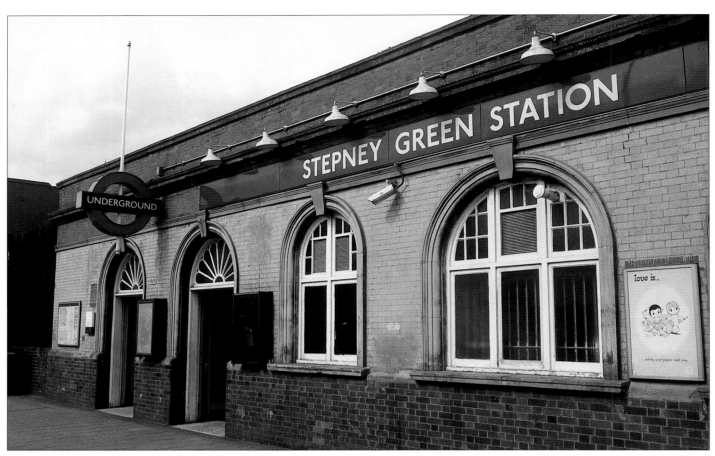

Left: Following the completion of the Circle and associated lines, the District Railway pressed on east with the Whitechapel & Bow Railway. This was in conjunction with the London, Tilbury & Southend Railway (LTSR), and a new station was built at **Stepney Green**. This was opened on 23 June 1902 and many original features remain. Designed by Ford, this is the smart surface building as it was on 29 March 2008.

Below left: Beyond Whitechapel, District steam-operated services to Barking and Upminster were inaugurated on 2 June 1902. At Campbell Road Junction (to the west of Bromley-by-Bow station) and where the District came to the surface, the services ran over the newly quadrupled LTSR tracks. These are the impressive station buildings on the bridge at **Plaistow** seen on 29 March 2008. The station had been used by the Tilbury Line's trains since 1858, but was rebuilt for the arrival of the District.

Above right: Inside **Plaistow** station, this is the view looking along the footbridge interior with its glazed roof on 24 December 1996. From this, stairs descend to platforms on the eastbound side (in distance) and to the westbound.

Centre right: The platforms at **Plaistow** were photographed on 29 March 2008. As can be seen, the westbound platform from which the picture is taken has the unusual feature of a succession of arches under the canopy, used today as locations for passenger seats.

Right: **Plaistow** is the home of a few very long station seats, seen here on 29 March 2008. These bear the initials LTSR of their former railway company owner on their end legs. 'Former' as, apart from Barking, this and all the other stations between Bromley-by-Bow (inclusive) and Upminster (exclusive) were transferred to the control of London Underground on 1 January 1969.

Left: **East Ham** station was also rebuilt for the District and this impressive and lengthy frontage at street level survives. Inside, the ticket hall is equally vast. Underground trains first called here in 1902 and it was photographed on 12 July 2005.

Right: This is the view of **East Ham** platforms, looking west with a D stock train departing on 29 March 2008. The neat valancing to the edge of the canopies is a welcome survivor. None of the stations which are now served only by the Underground retain public access to what may remain of their platforms on the down Tilbury lines.

Left: The railway at **Hounslow Central** station is above ground level to the left, and access is via this District Railway building dating from when the line was doubled in 1912. The station opened on 1 April 1886 as Heston-Hounslow, receiving its present name on 1 December 1925. Piccadilly Line services began on 13 March 1933 and ran in parallel with the District until the latter were discontinued on 9 October 1964. This well-restored station to a design by Harry Ford is seen on 26 June 2008.

Above: There is not much to be said about this unexciting entrance to **Ravenscourt Park** station, seen here on 11 March 2008, other than that it is functional in the way that stations should be. It was opened as Shaftesbury Road by the London & South Western Railway (LSWR) on 1 April 1873, with District trains first calling on 1 October 1877. The LSWR made its last appearance in 1906, since when usage has been by the Underground only.

Right: The fine roofs on the two island platforms at **Ravenscourt Park** District line were installed in 1911. This is the one on the westbound side (Platforms 3 & 4) seen from the approach steps leading from the ticket office on 11 March 2008. Although there are platforms on the Piccadilly Line tracks, none of the trains call.

Above: Chiltern Court at **Baker Street** was perhaps the magnum opus of Charles Clark, the Metropolitan Railway's architect. It is situated on the north side of the Marylebone Road at its junction with Baker Street. Completed in 1928, this huge block of high class flats has railway station requirements on the ground floor and below. Notably, these include what is now the Metropolitan Bar with its ornate ceiling, formerly the station tea rooms. The complex spans only the curved connection between the Metropolitan main line and that of the Circle and its construction was undertaken in conjunction with the remodelling of the station track layout in the years preceding. The date is 21 May 2008.

Left: The two sides of the Metropolitan at **Baker Street** are illustrated by this gateway, dating from about 1930. Passing through from this side gives access to services to King's Cross, Liverpool Street, Moorgate and Whitechapel. The company war memorial is partly obscured by the word 'Moorgate', and a C stock train is visible beyond on 21 May 2008.

Above: The other side of the **Baker Street** gateway offers Wembley, Harrow, Uxbridge, Watford and Amersham as destinations, or the heart of Metroland. This view too was photographed on 21 May 2008.

Below: At **Baker Street** are the Allsop Place company offices, which project over part of the main line platforms. This view of 21 May 2008 shows the through platform no 2 and an A stock train in no 1, one of the two bays. Despite the constrained location, the platforms have plenty of natural light, and passengers are protected from the weather by canopies.

Left: This is **Willesden Green** on 9 April 2008 at platform level, looking towards Baker Street. The island platform serves the Jubilee Line and, although there are platforms on all four lines here, Metropolitan trains as in the one seen approaching do not stop. The décor features green and blue mosaic tiles. It was not until this 1925 rebuilding that electric lighting was added, despite the electrification of the railway having taken place twenty years earlier.

Below: The platform facilities at **Willesden Green** feature a waiting room (which is open) and a clock above (showing the right time) at this nicely turned out station. Lighting of this area is enhanced by the thoughtful provision of skylights in the canopy. It is 28 June 2008.

Left: **Great Portland Street** is a circular building on its own traffic island, and is viewed here from the south side on 7 May 2008. It was one of the original Metropolitan Railway stations and was opened on 10 January 1863 as Portland Road. It has received a typical Charles Clark cream terracotta street-level reconstruction, dating from 1930. Despite appearances, the tree is beyond and not in the centre of the building.

Left: **Willesden Green** was an early station of the expanding Metropolitan Railway on its route to Harrow, opening on 24 November 1879. It was an important station as it was in a key position for the Willesden Park Estate. Enlargement of the facilities followed, and it was intended that it become an interchange station with the Great Central services. This never materialised, but the whole was rebuilt in 1925 to the well-known designs of Charles Clark. This lengthy station frontage with its two entrances is seen here on 26 June 2008. It features his faience style of tin-coloured earthenware to simulate stonework. He added the first floor to give the station prominence and this consisted of three residential flats. How refreshingly different from burying the station entrance, unseen, deep in a shopping centre!

Left: The fortunes of Wembley were linked to its importance as a sporting and entertainment centre. The main entrance to **Wembley Park** station is on the road over the railway and is seen here on 9 April 2008. The station frontage was reconstructed by the Metropolitan Railway in 1923 in anticipation of the crowds for sporting fixtures and the British Empire Exhibition of 1924/5. The building was renovated in 2005. This was the first example of Clark's more domestic style, as developed later at stations such as Stanmore.

Below left: The 1923 work at **Wembley Park** made provision for two extra platforms and the generally substantial nature of this station is seen with a northbound Jubilee Line train approaching on 18 April 1998. As a location, Wembley is well connected by three different railway lines, serving also Wembley Stadium and Wembley Central, and all of which continue to other destinations. Contrast this with Heathrow, whose two railways are mildly awkward dead-end extensions from a previously existing network.

Above right: The creation of the housing in what became known as Metroland and on which the fortunes (or at least the revenues) of the Metropolitan Railway depended, was accompanied by the building of extra stations where needed. Thus at the opening of the line to Uxbridge in 1904, the only intermediate station west of Harrow was Ruislip. The other six followed later, one of them being **Ruislip Manor** which was opened as a halt on 5 August 1912. That proved a little ambitious, and it was closed again between 1917 and 1919. Development only started properly in 1926. The modest platform facilities are seen here looking east towards Rayners Lane on 18 April 1998.

Centre right: **Stanmore** station building was photographed on 9 April 2008. This was designed by Charles Clark for the Metropolitan Railway, whose trains served it when it opened on 10 December 1932. This was a traditional-style station with brick walls and a central gable. There are dormer windows over the entrance which has shops each side, and a tiled roof with chimney stacks. The open air platforms are reached by stairs. Bakerloo Line trains replaced those of the Metropolitan from 20 November 1939 only to be replaced themselves by those of the Jubilee Line on 1 May 1979.

Right: At **Canons Park** Jubilee Line, there are two entrances from the street, each side of the bridge carrying the trains across the road. It is 7 May 2008. The station was built by the Metropolitan Railway and opened on 10 December 1932, initially for its own trains. Visually, it is not an exciting building.

LONDON UNDERGROUND STATIONS

Left: The ticket office at **Canons Park** was photographed on 7 May 2008, showing a very basic but adequate area, as long as queues do not build up. The stairs on the left lead to the northbound platform. The lack of staff is confirmed by the ticket barriers being left open.

Below left: Further infilling of Metroland required a new station at **Northwood Hills**, opened on 13 November 1933. This was the last station to be designed by the Metropolitan's 'Clarkitecht', as he was known by the Chairman, Lord Aberconway. The completion of the station came after the formation of the Board. In recent times, the space for a retail unit to the right of the entrance was crudely filled in as part of the work needed to install the Underground Ticketing System. The date is 26 April 2008.

Above: Generations of commuters knew the long slog at **Bank**, for years the only means of exit from the Waterloo & City Line opened on 8 August 1898. Using this tunnel, it was up a few steps, then a short walk, up a few steps, then a short walk, all the way to the top. This was the cue for the introduction of the Travelator situated in the adjoining shaft, which ground into action in 1960. The steps option remains for those who wish to use it and is seen here from the lower end on 29 March 2008.

Left: The Central London Railway (CLR) ran from Shepherd's Bush to Bank, and **Holland Park** is a relatively complete original station. This part of today's Central Line opened on 30 July 1900. It was the work of the architect Harry Bell Measures (1862-1940), using a part-baked but unglazed terracotta which resulted in a light-brown finish. All the stations had lift access to the platforms. The station roof here is no longer flat, as built, since new lifts in the 1980s required the hump which can be seen in this view of 29 March 2008.

Left: The exterior of **Queensway** CLR station of 30 July 1900 is seen here on 26 April 2008. It also retains the original external finish. This detailed view shows the lighting and ornamentation to the right of and above the station entrance. As can be seen, this station acquired additional commercial premises above it.

Above: The concentric rings described in the tunnel roof are typical of the Yerkes tube stations, of which **Regent's Park** is but one. This view is taken looking north towards Baker Street on 6 June 2000. The frieze is slightly above head height, alternating the station name with a brown Bakerloo Line roundel. This was a later system-wide application for tube tunnels, and helps passengers on the train identify the station. Before this, a good clue could be had for those in the know from the colour of the tiles. Camden Town, for instance, was (and is) a delicate powder blue.

Right: There is no necessity to provide surface buildings for tube stations, as long as the station entrance is clearly marked. This is **Regent's Park** Bakerloo Line on 7 May 2008. Stairs from each direction lead to a modest underground concourse and ticket office from which lifts take one to a level above the platforms, which themselves are at slightly different levels. The last bit is by stairs. The line was opened from Lambeth North to Baker Street on 11 March 1906.

Below: Station names may change over time, but also in the way they are spelt. **Regent's Park** is rendered thus along the frieze, but the tiled name keeps to the original Regents Park without the apostrophe. It is 7 May 2008.

Above: A Piccadilly Line station was built in suburban North London where Highbury Hill made a T-junction with Gillespie Road. Opened on 15 December 1906, the station was named after the latter. It is, however, only a short walk from here to Arsenal football ground. The station name was changed to **Arsenal** in 1932, and that association has required substantial works. Thus the station entrance was doubled in width through the acquisition of the adjacent house. This is the exterior with its huge roundel (plus a junior one) on 21 May 2008.

Right: These are the final steps up from the trains before the ticket office area at **Arsenal** is reached, seen here on 21 May 2008. This shows the UTS gates blocking your way and the help point on the left – or where you go to pay your fare before you escape through the barriers, if you haven't paid already.

Above: **Caledonian Road** is seen on 26 April 2008. This is a fine example of a station by Leslie Green (1875-1908), architect to the Underground Electric Railways of London (UERL group) and who has over 50 stations to his credit. His turned out to be a sadly short life, a result of overwork. The entrance and exit are now in the centre of the building, belying the 'Exit' information given above the locked doors on the right. It is rather larger than is now required, resulting in the commercial lettings shown. This Piccadilly Line station was opened on 15 December 2006.

Below left: It wasn't only the station names that were included in the tiles, and this Way Out sign with an arrow is a typical example. This happens to be at **Caledonian Road**, but similar versions in a colour to match that of the station tiling are commonplace at Leslie Green stations. It is 26 April 2008.

Below right: The shortest distance between any two London Underground stations is the 260m between Leicester Square and **Covent Garden**, seen here on 10 April 2008. This is a very constrained site and much ingenuity has gone into making the most of the facilities here. Some years ago, the area was decaying and consideration was being given to closure; now with the development of the former market it is exceedingly busy. This is an example of a Green station which has been built over; other features will be familiar.

Left: The 'Hampstead tube' as it became know colloquially had one station in the open air, at **Golders Green**. Opened on 22 June 1907, the tracks here are elevated, though the next station to the south, Hampstead, is still the deepest on the system at 59m below ground level. It is only 2km 35m distant, though part of Hampstead Heath lies in between. Golders Green station, seen here from the forecourt on 3 March 2008, has had substantial work carried out on it, notably for the installation of the Underground Ticketing System. The arched entrance is not original, as can be seen from its slightly different brick colour from that of the building behind.

Right: This is platform level at **Golders Green** on 3 March 2008 looking south with the tunnels (to Morden) in the distance. This shows the single track arrangement for the centre one of three, with an island platform each side. Generally, the centre track is useful for trains terminating here as opposed to running through to Edgware. The station is well protected from the elements.

Left: This elaborate double-sided platform bench-type seat with a vertical back is one of several similar to be found at **Golders Green**. It is perhaps more stylish than comfortable, and was seen on 3 March 2008.

Above: This is the view of **Hampstead** southbound platform looking north towards Golders Green on 3 March 2000. The treatment is similar to that of Regent's Park, and the use of the same architect certainly produced a unity of appearance between the three Yerkes lines. A feature which was only adopted later was the suicide pit between the running rails and below the return conductor rail. Any individual who for whatever reason falls onto the track has a greater chance of escaping injury from a train by rolling into this space.

Below: The original name of this station was to be Heath Street in which it is situated, but when it opened on 22 June 1907 it was named **Hampstead**. Once such decisions are made and committed to tiles, there is little scope for alteration. This view was taken over a century later on 3 March 2008.

Above: **Belsize Park** Northern Line station of 1907, photographed on 7 May 2008, is situated midway up Haverstock Hill. This climbs from the south at Chalk Farm and continues to rise towards Hampstead. This is also a Leslie Green station.

Right: All of Leslie Green's stations had a number of features in common. Perhaps most noticeable immediately was the use of shiny dark-red tiles in a colour popularly known as ox-blood around a steel framework. The latter was introduced to enable the subsequent construction of commercial premises above, though this never happened here, at **Chalk Farm** (1907). This is the most extensive of Green's façades, stretching as it does along two roads at this diverging junction. The use of semi-circular arches for windows is another feature, and all are seen here on 3 March 2008.

Above: Moving in closer, this is the **Chalk Farm** station entrance complete with Underground signage of two different eras and the neatly applied station name, on 3 March 2008.

Left: The entrances to **Warwick Avenue** station are to be found one each side of a wide Clifton Gardens. They lead to a subsurface ticket hall below. Between the two station entrances is the now relatively rare feature of a taxi drivers' shelter. Because cab drivers weren't allowed to leave their vehicles when parked at a stand, it was difficult for them to get a hot meal while at work. These distinctive small green huts were constructed by and are still run by the Cabmen's Shelter Fund, a charity established in London in 1875. The police did not allow the huts to be any larger than a horse and cart, as they stood on the public highway. Only 13 of the 61 built originally still exist. It is 7 May 2008.

Above: **Maida Vale**, Bakerloo Line, has one of the most interesting station entrances on the Underground network. A set of stairs with fine railings leads the intending passenger down to the subsurface ticket hall; this is the view to be had looking back up towards the entrance and The Kiosk. All is very much in the original condition of 6 June 1915 when it was opened. This view was that of 7 May 2008.

Below left: Enamel signs on the wall opposite the point at which they arrive on the platform greet passengers with a list of the destinations served by trains from there. This is one of the older styles of signs at **Maida Vale** on 7 May 2008. It is sandwiched between two signs giving the station name and of such a height that they can be seen through the car windows. The names of Trafalgar Square and Charing Cross have both been changed in the life of this sign, but unfortunately the replacement was not centred very accurately.

Below right: A version of the Underground roundel laid out in mosaics is, to say the least, decidedly rare – yet here at **Maida Vale** there are two of them. Well out of harm's way, they may be found each side of the entry stairwell; this one was photographed on 7 May 2008.

Above: The Bakerloo was extended northwards from Edgware Road to Queens Park, where it joined the London & North Western Railway on the surface. This work was completed in stages all the way to Watford Junction between 1913 and 1917. **Kilburn Park** was opened on 31 January 1915. It represents a distinct development of the Leslie Green architectural approach by Stanley A. Heaps, with the building overall of a lesser height as there was no lift gear to accommodate. The arches have been flattened accordingly. It is seen on 7 May 2008.

Below: This view is of the area at the top of the **Kilburn Park** escalators on 7 May 2008. The Queens Park extension was one of the first sections of tube to be built from new with escalators rather than lifts. Consequently, the lower landings are at platform level, rather than a higher level for lifts with the last section to the platforms being completed by stairs.

Above: **East Acton** is one of those modest small stations which one hardly expects to find. Opened on 3 August 1920 as part of the Central London's extension to Ealing Broadway, covered steps lead down from the station's two side platforms to the ticket office. This is situated in a quiet street, next to the road overbridge. It is 9 March 2008.

Below: At platform level at **East Acton**, the neat period waiting shelter is part of the original 1920 station and a several people have gathered for the approaching eastbound train of 1992 stock on 27 March 1995.

Left: First station north of the Morden terminus is **South Wimbledon**, where the shape of the roadway takes the form of a graceful curve, and the station frontage follows this faithfully. Wrote Pick: 'A station is an inviting doorway, in an architectural setting that cannot be missed by the casual pedestrian'. The material used is Portland stone, chosen partly for its ability to wash itself clean from pollution and other stains or tarnishing. Its success at this can best be judged by the reader. It is 22 April 2008.

Below: **Oval** station opened with the rest of the first stage of the City & South London Railway on 16 December 1890, and was subsequently closed for reconstruction 1923-4. The frontage as seen on 7 May 2008 uses the same general approach as others on the route to Morden, but the dimensions of the portion above the doorway are more like those at Kennington. Also of note is the long canopy which stretches the full length of the building; this station has recently been updated to produce the present result.

Above: The Edgware extension from Golders Green was eventually constructed and opened in sections. That to **Hendon Central** was commissioned on 19 November 1923, and was for a time the only new station. The station is situated at the busy Central Circus on the A41 and boasts a frontage with a series of stone columns. It was quickly built over as was indeed intended; it is very similar to Brent Cross, which remains as built. Hendon Central was the work of Stanley A. Heaps, who had been Leslie Green's assistant. After Green's death, he was appointed in 1910 architect to the UERL and in 1933 to a similar position with the London Passenger Transport Board. The station is seen here on 7 May 2008.

Right: **Burnt Oak**, also a Heaps station, was opened on 27 October 1924. Like Hendon Central, a street-level entrance leads to a footbridge from which steps descend to an open-air island platform with a substantial canopy. The large station name is in what has become known as the 'tombstone' variety. Mildly unfortunate perhaps, but once one has heard such a description there is no forgetting it. This is the scene looking south on 7 May 2008.

Left: Through their general design and the application of roundels and similar, Underground stations are usually very obvious to the stranger in search of their location. **Edgware**, seen here on 7 May 2008, is one of the rare exceptions, its frontage having a vaguely municipal appearance. Is this perhaps the local swimming baths? Edgware is a Stanley Heaps design and a passageway leads from the ticket office area onto a footbridge, with stairs descending to the platforms. The station was built at what is now the permanent end of the Northern Line and opened on 18 August 1924.

Below: The train shed at **Edgware** clearly covers two platforms only, nos 2 & 3. Platform 1, from which this view was taken on 7 May 2008, is by contrast uncovered. The 1935-40 New Works Programme envisaged the Underground being extended the three miles to Bushey Heath. An additional feeder line would have been that of the LNER via Mill Hill East, taken over and electrified. In the event, work was suspended in 1941 and subsequently abandoned. Post-war Green Belt legislation meant that further housing development would not take place, so the need for a railway to serve it also evaporated.

Above: This view taken on 7 May 2008 is of Platforms 1 & 2 at **Edgware**, beneath the rather fine overall roof. In the distance the bridge under Station Road which would have taken the Northern Line on towards Bushey Heath can just be seen.

Below: The projection of District Line trains beyond Barking ceased in 1905, to be resumed with the building of a second pair of tracks through to Upminster. From 12 September 1932, **Dagenham East** saw Underground electric trains on the slow lines set aside for their use. This is the view of the station building from the street on 10 April 2008. It is an LMS design (and indeed was that company's property), typical of the stations on the extension.

Above: Today, **Dagenham East** is very well turned out, as this picture of 29 March 2008 shows. Although only Underground trains have used the station for many years, the platforms on the main LTS line are still more or less intact. As can be seen here, a solid fence divides the westbound District from the down LTS line. There are, however, locked gates in between, so its use is not ruled out altogether.

Below: At **Elm Park**, the connection from street to the (island) platform is by ramp, seen here on 29 March 2008. This does not pose a problem for the mobility-impaired, although it is a long run for those who find they are a little late for the train they intend to catch. Consequently, high-speed collisions with those alighting and struggling up the slope are not impossible.

Above right: The island platform at **Elm Park** seen here looking west on 29 March 2008 is tremendously wide. This is helped by the central pillars supporting the canopy, which result in the platform being almost entirely unobstructed. The downside is the separation required for the District Line tracks on each side, which can cause alignment problems should higher speeds be required. Here, this is most unlikely.

Right: This is the ticket office at **Upminster Bridge** on 29 March 2008. This new station was opened on 17 December 1934, again by the LMS as one of their stations, but only ever used by the Underground. This is the one station on the extension from Barking to have the station building below track level, reached by the subway beyond the automatic ticket barriers. One of these has been left open due to there being no staff in attendance.

Right: **Cockfosters** is certainly a Charles Holden classic; there are three tracks with four platform faces, symmetrically arranged under this impressive roof photographed on 10 April 2008. Of particular note is the departure clock, though its message is now given by the modern indicators.

Below right: Trains in the platforms at each side at **Cockfosters** are relatively hidden, looking towards buffer stops on 10 April 2008. The whole, though, makes excellent use of natural light.

Above: **Cockfosters** station was opened as the northern terminal of the Piccadilly Line on 31 July 1933. This platform roundel in a concrete frame shows dimensional differences in the width of the bar, but remains unmistakable for what it is. The date is 25 May 2001.

Below: Steps rise from the below ground-level **Cockfosters** platforms to each side of the A111 main road. Those wanting buses going north follow the appropriate subway and surface in what might be described as an extended bus shelter with lay-by. It is 10 April 2008.

Left: Sir Hugh Casson, later to become Director of Architecture for the Festival of Britain, described Charles Holden's **Arnos Grove** as: 'A perfect example of functionalism; a complete synthesis of the modern and the traditional and an effective answer to those who object that modern architecture is characterless'. It is certainly one of Holden's finest buildings; the new station was opened to traffic on 19 September 1932. This view of the drum and its supporting base was taken on 24 April 1997.

Right: This elegant and distinctive platform-seat design incorporating the sign for the station name is seen here at **Arnos Grove** on 24 April 1997, but similar ones were later to be found all over the system. Over the years they have been removed and sometimes replaced, but have more recently made a comeback as other illustrations in this book will show.

Left: **Turnpike Lane** lies at what is now a busy crossroads. Part of the Piccadilly Cockfosters extension, the station was opened on 19 September 1932. This Holden creation incorporates a bus station (out of sight behind), but the facilities for trams are long gone. The heavily louvred openings in the towers provide high-level intake for the tube ventilation plant, and help to integrate them visually with the building below. This 10 April 2008 view shows the main building, but what is not apparent is the depth of the ticket office. The floor of this is 3.7m below street level and reached by stairs. Thus there is level access to the subways, but natural light from the large windows is retained.

Right: Additional entrances to the station at **Turnpike Lane** via subways includes this robust set of steps down from Turnpike Lane itself, photographed on 10 April 2008. The station name, it will be noted, is not in Piccadilly Line blue.

Left: For some reason, the subway entrance at Duckett's Corner to **Turnpike Lane** station was completely covered. It was photographed on 10 April 2008, complete still with original 'Tickets & Trains' signage.

Left: This is the lower-level landing at **Turnpike Lane** on 21 May 2008, showing the pair of uplighters. Platforms are to the left and right, and the escalators are behind the camera. Frank Pick expressed himself well pleased with the overall result. In a letter to the chief engineer, he referred to the station as 'a group of buildings that is a credit to our undertaking'.

Below: A feature of the platforms at **Turnpike Lane** is the series of ventilation grilles found above alternate station-name roundels. Each of these show toll houses for the turnpike, with a horse and rider approaching from the left, and a pair of heavy horses from the right. They are the work of Harold Stabler and were photographed on 10 April 2008.

Left: 'The circular ticket hall at **Chiswick Park**, District Line, rises in a splendid sweep above a lower rectangular structure. A small tower has been introduced, intended no doubt to make the building more visible from the main Chiswick High Road. It serves the practical purpose of a signpost'. Thus Christian Barman, Pick's biographer. The station platforms are on a viaduct, the ticket hall drum being wedged somewhat uncomfortably between the railway and a busy road junction. There had been a station on this site since 1879, but the Holden reconstruction was completed in 1932. This picture was taken on 11 March 2008.

Right: The Warwick Road entrance to **Earl's Court** station was reconstructed in 1937 together with a separate below-ground access direct to the Exhibition site. This 25 May 2001 view shows one of the smaller examples of Charles Holden's work from the Exhibition forecourt.

Left: As with other railways, some Underground platforms are very exposed to the elements. This affects particularly those raised on viaducts or bridging above ground level. These are the waiting facilities on the eastbound District Line platforms at **Chiswick Park**; the shelter provides a relatively secluded area on 11 March 2008, without being remote from the action.

Left: **Park Royal** station, opened on 1 March 1936, has the characteristic Holden-style tower, although designed by Felix Lander. A large roundel dominates the scene in this view from the eastbound platform on 29 June 2008. The circular ticket office area with its row of high level windows will be noted, giving the whole building a light and airy interior. The layered steps to the platforms likewise provide plenty of natural light, while the waiting area at platform level is integral with the bottom of the steps.

Left: The connection between the ticket office area and the platforms can sometimes be a design weak spot. Each is fine, but sometimes the join shows. At **Park Royal**, this footbridge leads to stairs down to each of the two platforms which are located in a cutting. This fully integrated design was pictured on 26 April 2008.

Right: **Sudbury Town** station opened originally on 28 June 1903. It was later to be the site of the original 'brick box with concrete lid', designed by Charles Holden, whose station building replaced the previous offering. Seen here from the street side on 29 June 2008, this is the main building on the eastbound platform, opened on 19 July 1931. In the description by Holden's biographer Eitan Karol, 'The station is dominated by the booking hall, a tall space almost twice as high as it is wide, giving it the proportions of a chapel rather than a station. It is a beautifully proportioned space, where every element is crafted and considered.'

Right: The passimeter was once widely installed on stations in the London area, both by the LNER and London Transport. It had the advantage of the same clerk being able both to issue tickets (on one side) and to collect them (on the other). Swinging barriers controlling entry to and exit from the platform could be fastened from inside. That at **Sudbury Town**, seen here on 22 March 2003, has been replaced by UTS but is still in situ.

Below: This is the eastbound platform at **Sudbury Town**, seen here from the westbound on 26 April 2008. The curved passenger waiting areas are prominent in this view; they are not waiting rooms, as there are no doors. Note also the very capacious canopy.

Above: At the end of the Metropolitan (and Piccadilly) branch to **Uxbridge** lies a station which in many ways mimics Cockfosters of five years earlier. Opened on a new site much more convenient for the town centre on 4 December 1938, the station is presently being upgraded. This view of 26 April 2008 shows the main street entrance in front of what was once the turning circle for trolleybuses. The upturned wheels-with-leaf-springs designs are by Joseph Armitage; the gap between them allows the stained glass display inside the station to be illuminated by daylight.

Below: Within **Uxbridge** station can be found this vivid stained-glass display by Ervin Bossanyi featuring the coats of arms of Uxbridge Urban District Council. Each side (not shown) are those of the counties of Middlesex and Buckinghamshire. It was pictured on 27 February 2003 but cannot be viewed during the present refurbishment.

Above: **Northfields** station was rebuilt on a new site and was opened on 19 May 1932. According to Barker & Robbins, the station building became a hall, and not a house. In their view, the style combined geometrical forms, horizontal canopies and bold fenestration with great elegance. The station has two island platforms reached by stairs. It was photographed on 22 March 2003.

Right: The **Northfields** ticket office area features uplighters, which rather incongruously offer a halo effect from the devices designed to prevent birds perching on them. The generally bright and welcome nature of the whole area as seen here on 22 March 2003 can be observed.

Above: The station at **Boston Manor** opened on 1 May 1883, and was totally reconstructed in the Holden idiom. As Barman described it, 'we find fresh experiments with a slim decorative column standing on a tower block of less height, as on a pedestal'. Work was completed on the station on 25 March 1934; it is seen here on 24 May 2004.

Below left: This is **Boston Manor** from the westbound platform level looking east on 24 May 2004. The tower still dominates, but the traditional (and very large) canopies mark out the platform area as being of a far more typical railway station appearance.

Below right: The Underground station name of **Osterley** is displayed on a concrete panel between two posters, with a lamp standard above to ensure that the latter can be read after dark. This is part of the detailed design which graces many stations. It is 22 March 2003.

Right: **Hounslow West** was completed on 5 July 1931; it is seen here on 24 May 2004. This was one of the later Holden versions of his designs for the Morden extension, this time featuring shop units within the frontage of the building. The area immediately outside is used for buses.

Left: There are some notable features at **Hounslow West**. Thus the moulded ticket hall ceiling for which Basil Ionides was responsible has seven sides, matched by the chandelier seen in this view of 28 June 2008. The roundel can be seen in the window patterns.

Right: The ticket office area itself at **Hounslow West** has some notable tiled frieze work, again by Basil Ionides. Alas, not all is quite as it seems. It was once a terminal station with platforms on the surface, but the construction of the Heathrow extension required a new alignment for the tracks and platforms below ground level. These are situated a considerable distance further away from the station building. Thus the passenger now has to walk through a rather nasty enclosed tin box situated in what is now a car park, to reach the top of the stairs down.

Left: The rounded ends to the buildings and canopies on the island platforms at **Harrow-on-the-Hill** are a typical feature of the 1938-9 period when it was reconstructed. The Metropolitan line station at this, the capital city of Metroland, dates from 2 August 1880 when it was a terminus. Another five years passed before the main line was extended to, initially, Pinner. It is 26 April 2008.

Right: Where traffic growth so prompts, station platforms can be lengthened. This can be relatively straightforward or may require much additional work. On the Central London the stations were built on humps, to slow arriving trains and accelerate those departing with the help of gravity in each case. Platform lengthening from 325ft to 427ft would allow 8-car trains to be run, and the work was carried out entirely during a series of night engineering possessions during 1937-8. The results of this work can still be seen in the slightly irregular finishes to the platform tunnels as in this view of **Queensway** of 10 April 2008.

Left: Harold Stabler was responsible for a series of decorative tiles installed on some station platforms in the late 1930s. This one, of the London Passenger Transport Board's headquarters at 55 Broadway, is at **St Paul's**. A total of 18 different designs have been recorded; examples can be seen here and at other Underground stations rebuilt in this era. While the tile could have been cleaner when photographed on 18 August 2003, a little bit of dirt does help show up the detail.

Left: The Bakerloo's, now Jubilee's, **Swiss Cottage** excels in its escalators, seen here from the lower landing on 9 April 2008. The uplighters have been retained and the whole scene has altered little from when they were installed 70 years ago except, that is, for the lighting level, which here and at many other Underground locations is now at much greater intensity than it was in days past.

Right: The station at **West Acton** Central Line was reconstructed and opened in November 1940, setting a rather different tone. It is the work of Brian Lewis. The main building, seen here on 9 March 2008, has a brick wall either side, with a large window area and canopy at the front. This replaced the original Great Western station, opened on 5 November 1923.

Left: From the westbound platform, **West Acton** shows the covered waiting areas integral with the bottom of the stairways on 9 March 2008. The windows at this side of the station building afford a useful visual guide to passengers to check if their train is arriving and whether they need to hurry down the steps.

Left: Plans were prepared by Charles Holden to rebuild **Finchley Central** Northern Line with two island platforms, but this work never progressed beyond the very early stages. It thus remains largely as it was with a single southbound Platform 3, shown here on 23 June 2003. One difficulty in the substitution of tube trains for those of ordinary railways is the change in the ideal platform height. Finchley Central had these lowered, with the result that the stairs down to platform level stopped short of where they are required. That has to be compensated for by the introduction of a ramp, as seen here. Individual circumstances can make such work more or less difficult (and costly); the problems of changing platform levels if escalators are involved are clearly in a different league.

Right: The originator of the Underground diagram of lines as we know it today was Harry Beck (1903-1974), a draughtsman for the LPTB. He realised that maps to scale or approximately so were unlikely to produce a readable result, given that the system was fast expanding at the time. Thus he depicted them in diagrammatic form which, with some misgivings, the Board eventually adopted. This was in 1932, and Beck's creation and its descendents have been with us ever since. This plaque at **Finchley Central** seen on 3 March 2008 relates to his being a local resident, though West Finchley is much nearer to where he actually lived. Perversely, present management refers to today's computer-drawn version as a Tube map. It isn't just the Tube lines which it covers, and it certainly isn't a map. Ah well!

IN MEMORY OF
HARRY BECK
THE ORIGINATOR OF THE
DISTINCTIVE LONDON UNDERGROUND MAP
WHO LIVED NEAR HERE AND USED
THE STATION REGULARLY
THE MAP IS USED BY MILLIONS DAILY
AND HAS BECOME RECOGNISED
AS A CLASSIC
WORLD-WIDE

Left: The familiar roundel at **Woodside Park**, displaying the yellow brick on which it is placed, 24 April 1997.

Left: This is **Woodside Park** Northern Line station with its somewhat austere appearance, displaying its Great Northern antecedents. This is situated on the up side of the line (GNR terminology, Southbound in LU). Notable is the use of the yellow brick favoured by that company, no doubt conveyed by it from the brickworks at Fletton, near Peterborough.
The wall-mounted pillar box carries the VR insignia; unusual for what is now a tube line. Although often referred to as being Victorian, the tube network proper is largely an Edwardian creation. This view was taken on 29 June 2008.

Right: **Woodside Park** was opened by the Great Northern Railway in 1872 and was rebuilt in 1889. It is a fine example of a (since) little altered station of that company. The main station building and the usual offices as seen here on 24 April 1997 are on the up side and at ground level. Until the late 1950s, it even boasted a W. H. Smith bookstall. The former railway goods yard (beyond and out of sight) is used for car parking.

Left: The waiting shelter on the down side at **Woodside Park** is seen from the bottom of the footbridge steps to the up platform. As the bridge is open also to non-rail users, there is no segregation from passengers. This stems from the nearest alternative crossing of the railway being a road underbridge about 200m distant, and has the unusual effect of separating the station paid areas. Consequently, would-be rail users using the bridge will follow this route via the main building, where they will encounter a UTS barrier. It is 29 June 2008.

Left: The Underground is close to the surface at **Redbridge** Central Line station, opened on 14 December 1947, to the extent that construction is by cut-and-cover methods and access to the single island platform is by stairs. From this angle, the circular Holden ticket office is almost hidden; as the *Railway Gazette* commented, 'the tower with its supporting wings prevents the station from looking like an insignificant ventilating shaft, transformer kiosk or pump house'. This view was taken in December 1996.

Right: **Gants Hill** station is situated at a major five-way road intersection and the Central Line station is accessed by local authority subways to the ticket office below. This view of 29 March 2008 shows some of the large-scale provision that has been made, with ramps now as well as steps. The station was opened on 14 December 1947 as part of the postponed New Works Programme, although the uncompleted running tunnels had been used during the war as a munitions factory by the Plessey Co.

Left: The platforms at **Gants Hill** are reached by escalators. The large area between the platforms is occupied a low-level concourse 46m long with a barrel-vaulted ceiling. This is an early example of lighting mainly by fluorescent tubes, the result of which might be judged extremely effective. Short passageways off this area lead to the platforms on either side. Thus the Moscow Metro came to London. It is 29 March 2008.

Left: The eastbound platform at **Gants Hill** is straight and uses cream tiles with orange borders, giving a pleasing overall appearance. The date is 26 May 2001.

Right: The attention to detail at **Gants Hill** was remarkable, as shown by this London Transport clock and its use of roundels in lieu of figures on 26 May 2001.

Left: At platform level, **Newbury Park** Central Line is very much in keeping with other former Great Eastern stations on this line, but at street level there is a decided difference. This huge roof is in effect the local bus station, immediately adjacent to the present station entrance. It is large enough to accommodate double-deck buses and is situated adjacent to the A12 Eastern Avenue. A cosy location it is not! It was designed by Oliver Hill and opened on 6 July 1949. It is seen here in December 1996.

Right: **Barkingside** station was opened by the Great Eastern Railway on 1 May 1903. The reason for the ornate and very effective treatment of its main building complete with its smart little cupola on the roof is unclear, since the station serves only a modest-sized community on the western side of the line. To the east lies open land; in the early days, the station was closed from 1916 to 1919 due to lack of traffic. Still very much in the same form in which it was built, London Underground Central Line services commenced on 31 May 1948.

Regrettably, the combination of tree growth and the use of the modest forecourt area for car parking restrict the view that can be obtained of the main station building today. It is 29 March 2008.

Left: The business side of **Barkingside** station, as it were, is seen here from the westbound platform on 26 May 2001. All the usual trappings of a main-line station are present, with a capacious canopy to shelter what have inevitably always been modest numbers of travellers. Like many other Underground stations which were formerly owned by one of the main-line companies, it is well cared for.

Left: Platform canopies need support, and several railway companies used these as a means of displaying their ownership. Thus GER stands for Great Eastern Railway at **Barkingside**; it is 26 May 2001.

Right: **Chigwell** station platforms are situated in a deep and steep-sided cutting with the station building on Chigwell High Street, which spans the railway. It is of general Great Eastern rural station appearance and was opened on 1 May 1903, though it has been considerably modified over the years. Presumably, the white painted areas are designed to deter motorists trying to park from ramming the building. Underground trains started running here on 21 November 1948. This picture was taken on 29 March 2008.

Left: Long staircases lead down to the two side platforms at **Chigwell**, which are complete with period canopies and seats cantilevered out from the side walls. Here, somewhat perversely, eastbound trains are heading west and westbound trains east. However, passengers can get to London, which is due south west of here, by setting off in either direction! As can be seen, the whole is smartly turned out, with extremely lofty canopies. This platform view dates from 29 March 2008.

Left: Alone of the Great Eastern stations on the eastern end of the Underground's Central Line taken over in the late 1940s, **Loughton** station was completely reconstructed. This was necessary because of the selection of a new station site, further north. This brought it as close as possible to the centre of Loughton, but the embankment location meant that stairs would be needed from the street entrance level.

The new station was designed by John Murray Easton. The ticket hall uses semi-circular windows, made with square glass bricks in a reinforced concrete frame. This reflects the form of the ceiling inside and also presents a large illuminated area to the outside at night. This view of the outside of the station building, showing its affinity with King's Cross, was taken on 29 March 2008.

Below: There are three tracks at **Loughton**, served by four platform faces, a common Underground arrangement. The canopies are of reinforced concrete, cast in situ. Construction was sufficiently well advanced at the outbreak of war in 1939 that it was allowed to continue to completion, and the new station opened on 28 April 1940 for use by LNER steam services. The introduction of Underground trains was delayed until after the war, electric services as far as Loughton starting on 21 November 1948. At this stage, responsibility was transferred from what was then British Railways to London Transport. This view is of the southern end of the station, on 26 May 2001.

Right: **Theydon Bois** is a pleasant wayside station, which on 29 March 2008 had a splendid display of daffodils seemingly in every flowerbed. Again of Great Eastern origin, it was opened on 24 April 1865 as Theydon. Bois (for wood) was soon added. It became part of the Underground system on 25 September 1949.

Below: The tangle of the terminating arrangement in the Shepherds Bush area was finally resolved with the construction of the new **White City** station about 320m north of the previous Wood Lane. This opened its doors to traffic on 23 November 1947 and the platforms were constructed to take 8-car trains. It was designed by K. J. Seymour in the Holden style. There are three tracks separated by two island platforms. This allows terminating trains to reverse in the centre road and also keep flows of passengers separate. However, a unique feature is that right-hand running is practised here, which can lead to some confusion for the uninitiated. This view of the station building was taken on 11 July 2007.

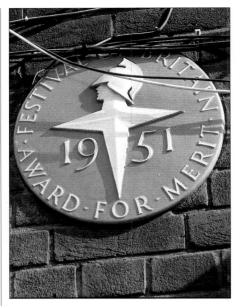

Above left: Few railway stations can be seen by quite so many motorists as the 'flying saucer' at **Hanger Lane**, which lies in the middle of a five-way road junction. Despite appearances, this is not a quiet location; there was just long enough for the photographer when the lights changed on 26 April 2008.

This station with its eye-catching 13.5m diameter dome was designed and constructed by the Great Western Railway. Access is by a number of local authority pedestrian subways which lead to the ticket office area and station entrance. Since the construction of the A40 underpass in 1960, there have been no other ways in. The single island platform is at ground level and reached by steps. It is largely in the open, despite being below the gyratory. Underground trains started running on 30 June 1947 and ownership was transferred to the London Transport Executive on 1 January 1948.

Centre left: **Greenford** station is situated at the junction of the National Railways branch from Ealing Broadway (the Greenford loop) and these trains terminate at the centre platform of this elevated station. This is the street view on 26 April 2008. The GWR local services running roughly parallel to the new Central Line extensions were in effect discontinued with the introduction of tube services here on 30 June 1947, though the GW/BR platforms at a lower level and beyond the Underground tracks did not close finally until 1963.

Left: The main station building is quite cavernous, as this view looking downward from the stairs shows. Only one escalator (up direction) is provided at **Greenford**, which occupies the position on the far left. There was formerly a route through to the GWR/BR platforms in the wall opposite, but this has long been bricked up. It is 26 April 2008.

Left: **White City** was an entirely post-war construction project; that it was clearly well thought of resulted in this Festival of Britain Award. This was photographed on 11 July 2007; it was still partly obscured by continuing reconstruction work in mid-2008.

Right: The widening of the Metropolitan from two to four tracks saw the additional tracks built on the west side of the existing station, which remains. This is **North Harrow** looking towards Amersham on 25 April 2008 with an A stock train arriving. There is a strong contrast between the original platform building and the later addition beyond. The station opened on 22 March 1915.

Centre right: The first station across the Hertfordshire boundary, **Moor Park**, is surrounded by golf clubs and playing fields. The station was comprehensively rebuilt with two island platforms serving all four tracks as part of the Amersham electrification. It was opened on 23 April 1961. This is the ticket office entrance at street level below, pictured on 18 April 1998. The original station here, known as Sandy Lodge, dated from 9 May 1910, making the final transition to its present name on 25 September 1950.

Below: Massive works at **Barking** were undertaken by British Railways before their 1962 electrification of the LTS line to remove grade conflicts as far as possible. These were between their own trains, including freight, and also with those of London Transport. A large brand-new station building in the style of the times was built across the tracks at street level with entrances at each end. It is seen here on 29 March 2008. The station was opened in 1961.

Above: **Bromley-by-Bow** station building stands on a bridge overlooking the platforms. It was gutted by fire on 20 February 1970 and was rebuilt by British Rail. This was a little odd, since the station had become London Transport property over a year earlier. The new building was opened 11 June 1972 and is seen here on 10 June 2003.

Below: The building of the Victoria Line started in 1963, when the emphasis was on functional buildings and the favourite colour seemed to be grey. As one of the objectives was to provide interchange with as many other railways and Underground lines as possible, completely new stations were a decided rarity. On the line originally authorised between Walthamstow Central and Victoria, **Blackhorse Road** which opened on 1 September 1968 was the only freestanding station out of 12. (The direct link to the Tottenham & Hampstead BR line came later). This external view of the station designed by Kenneth Seymour is dated 10 April 2008; the black horse is of cast iron. The detritus of local authority rubbish bins and bicycles chained to the railings here, as at so many other places, don't enhance the scene.

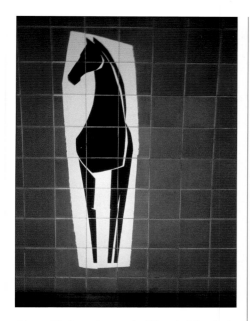

Above: Each station on the Victoria Line had a platform mural above the seats associated with the station concerned. Some of the more successful are illustrated here. The 'Black Horse' by Hans Unger is, of course, at **Blackhorse Road** and was pictured on 10 April 2008.

Above right: An attractive idea for **Tottenham Hale**, also opened on 1 September 1968, was to show a ferry on the Lea in days past. It was designed by Edward Bawden and photographed in October 1999.

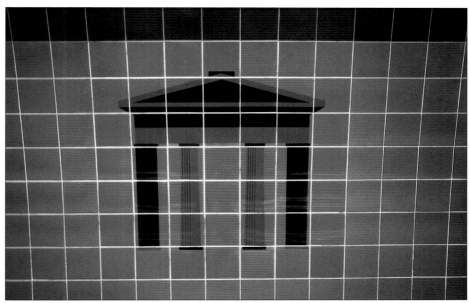

Centre right: Despite the efforts of Sir John Betjeman, the Doric Arch at **Euston** main line station was demolished. In the end, the decision so to do had to be taken by the then Prime Minister, Harold Macmillan. It lives on in the Underground in this design by Tom Eckersley. The Victoria Line station was opened on 1 December 1968; this picture was taken on 22 April 2008.

Right: The head of Queen Victoria was the obvious choice for the new line's symbolic representation at **Victoria**, opened on 7 March 1969. This too is the work of Edward Bawden. The photograph was taken on 22 April 2008.

Below: The coming of the Victoria Line to **Stockwell** as part of the Brixton extension was on 23 July 1971. This required the construction of two new platforms, which were arranged to give line-to-line cross-platform interchange to the Northern Line. The surface station building was completely rebuilt as seen here on 26 April 2008, though the slightly darker brown brick portions on the upper storey were added later. One commentator has described it as 'rather nondescript', which seems fair.

Left and this page: **Charing Cross** Northern Line platforms, which had latterly been known as Strand, were closed to traffic on 18 June 1973 for major reconstruction work. This was to link the station as an interchange with the Bakerloo and the initial Jubilee Line. It was reopened on 30 April 1979 by HRH Prince Charles, with public services commencing the following day. Each of the 107m Northern Line platforms was now adorned with a stunning mural created by David Gentleman, depicting rather earlier events. It was described as follows:

The original Charing Cross was built in 1291-1294 by Edward I in memory of his wife, Queen Eleanor of Castile. It was the most splendid of the twelve Eleanor Crosses erected to mark the successive places her body rested on its way from Lincoln to Westminster Abbey, and it stood near here until it was destroyed in 1647.

Richard of Crundale and Roger of Crundale were the master masons. The stone came from Corfe in Dorset and Caen in Normandy; Richard of Corfe and John of Corfe cut the English stone. Alexander of Abingdon and William of Ireland carved the statues of Queen Eleanor which stood halfway up the Cross, and Ralph of Chichester carved some of the decoration. Many others whose names are forgotten took part in the work: quarrymen, rough-hewers, masons, mortarers, layers, setters, carpenters, thatchers, scaffolders, labourers, falcon or crane-men, apprentices, hodmen, drivers, horsemen and boatmen.

Wrote Gentleman, 'The aim was to give some idea of the working lives and the skills of the craftsmen of the time and, in a way, to acknowledge our debt to them.'
The illustrations are much-enlarged prints from wood engravings on boxwood blocks, screen-printed onto the wall panels.

The mural is still in excellent condition, though the openings in it for litter and for staff letters are now blocked off. In the more stringent times which followed, the enforced lack of advertising revenue was regretted.

Above: **Borough**, seen here on 26 April 2008, was one of the former C&SLR 1890s stations, but the surface buildings today bear no resemblance to the original. The present building dates from the 1970s and is of striking appearance, its rounded nature emphasised by the external tiling. The concrete roundel on a post (with shadow!) is an unusual feature.

Right: The bottleneck caused by the four tracks south from Wembley Park to Finchley Road feeding into only two at that point was finally dealt with by the construction of a new line for the Bakerloo in tube from that point to Baker Street. This was opened on 20 November 1939. As one of the two intermediate stations then built, **Swiss Cottage** was given this tower in the late 1970s to act as a beacon for one of the subway entrances but also for ventilation purposes. No other surface buildings remain, with the other entrances being by stairways around this busy road junction. It was photographed on 9 April 2008.

Right: Sir Arthur Conan Doyle's detective Sherlock Holmes was known by all of his admirers to reside at 221b Baker Street, though the address too was fictional. The figure, complete with deerstalker hat and pipe, was, however, a fitting addition to the deep-level platforms at **Baker Street** station. This image is on the northbound Bakerloo platform, and was pictured on 21 May 2008.

Left: **Angel** station was built in 1901 and closed for the C&SLR reconstruction between 1922 and 1924. But it survived as one of the few with a central island platform and entrance/exit by a modest stairway at the northern end. This gave access to lifts to the surface. The station was getting busier and busier, to the extent that this was causing substantial difficulties for users. Consequently, the northbound Northern Line track was diverted in a new tunnel and two banks of escalators built, together with a station entrance on a new site, with work complete in 1992 after a period of closure. The new entrance is shown here on 3 March 2008.

Left: The Department of Transport's plan for building the M40 as a relief to the A40 to Oxford met with a problem where the new road was to pass below Metropolitan (and Piccadilly) tracks at **Hillingdon**. The result was the construction of a new station on embankment and slightly to the west. It was opened on 6 December 1992. This view shows the overall platform canopy, looking towards Uxbridge on 29 June 2008.

Below left: This long high-level walkway links the ticket office area at **Hillingdon** (right) with the street; the A40 is routed through the cut in the foreground. There is extensive ground-level station car-parking provision here, part of which can just be seen in this view of 29 June 2008.

Below: The street level view of the station building at **South Ealing** was taken on 24 May 2004. The station was opened on 1 May 1883 by the District Railway, though only Piccadilly Line trains have called since 1964. The ticket office area was rebuilt in this pleasing style together with the station footbridge in 1998.

Above: The ticket office area at **Hillingdon** is bright and airy, though the fabric of the station is beginning to show that it was built over 15 years ago. It is 29 June 2008.

Left: **Southwark** is a free-standing station on a corner site, the outside of which is seen here on 7 May 2008. It was designed by Richard MacCormac of MacCormac, Jamieson & Pritchard. This Jubilee Line station opened on 20 November 1999.

Below: There are two levels of concourse at **Southwark**. This, the higher of the two, features a high glass roof which allows daylight to enter the building and to form the patterns seen here. From this level, exit can be made either to the street or to a station with another name – Waterloo East. Passengers for the latter must hold a valid ticket for travel on National Rail or which will allow them to use that station's exit. Any Underground-only ticket will be swallowed up by the UTS gates on leaving Southwark. This photograph was taken on 7 May 2008.

Left: Jubilee Line construction saw the roundels on the platforms displayed generally in this manner. This is **Westminster** on 14 March 2001.

Left: While the subsurface lines (District and Circle) at **Westminster** are just that, access to the Jubilee introduces a further two levels since the westbound track is below the eastbound. The station complex was built using excavation rather than tunnel-boring methods, which has resulted in as many as 17 escalators linking the various levels, plus five lifts for the mobility-impaired and, of course, staircases. This view of 21 May 2008 gives an idea of the scale of this impressive installation.

Left: The lower-level concourse at **Southwark** features these striking beacons with stainless steel panels; again, the date is 7 May 2008.

Centre left: Platform doors have been installed at all below-ground stations on the Jubilee Line extension; these are at **Southwark** and were photographed on 24 December 1999. From the passengers' point of view they do inject some order into boarding and alighting, but standing back to let people alight (as instructed) still allows those so inclined to barge in quickly and grab the last seat. More prosaically, platform doors do assist ventilation and draught relief, while there are also safety benefits.

Below left: The descent to the island platform on the Jubilee line extension station at **Bermondsey** is by escalator in a shaft filled with natural light to create a feeling of spaciousness. The station was designed by Ian Ritchie Associates. This was the view on 7 May 2008.

Above right: The Jubilee Line platforms at **Canada Water** station opened on 17 November 1999, and for the East London Line two days later. At surface level is this 25m glass drum construction and daylight from this percolates to the station concourse 22m below ground level. The site is that of the former Albion Dock of the Surrey Commercial group, and this photograph was taken on 18 June 2003. There is an adjacent bus station.

Right: It was the prospects for the development of Canary Wharf which led to the Jubilee Line extension being diverted away from the City to run to Stratford via Docklands. This is the main entrance to Foster + Partners' **Canary Wharf** station as dusk falls on 19 February 2003. The station is 300m long and is situated in the remains of the former East India Dock. It opened on 17 September 1999. The position is not ideal and it is, notably, nearer Heron Quays station on the Docklands Light Railway than the DLR's Canary Wharf.

Left: A series of busy escalators takes passengers from the surface level at **Canary Wharf** down to ticket-office level, with another flight needed to reach the trains. The next Jubilee Line stations on each side are south of the river; Canary Wharf is north. That accounts for the depth needed. Given the expected future usage, the design principles were durability and ease of maintenance. It is 19 February 2003.

Right: A station seat on the **Canary Wharf** platforms is seen on 19 February 2003. This bears a certain resemblance to the Underground seats of an earlier era, as seen at Arnos Grove earlier in this book.

Left: The Jubilee Line ends at **Stratford** station, where large-scale works affecting also the National Rail and DLR parts of the station have been continuing for some years. Jubilee Line services at surface level commenced on 14 May 1999, using new platforms located to the west of the line from Canning Town to be used for DLR services in future. This is the totally rebuilt exterior of the station, operated by National Express East Anglia and seen here on 29 March 2008. Central Line services also use Stratford, but they are at high level, where they offer cross-platform interchange with local main-line services.

Right: The Underground Ticketing System (UTS) gates are everywhere. Passengers either 'touch in' with an Oystercard (Smartcard) using the yellow targets which can be seen on top of the gate mechanism, or feed a conventional credit-card-sized ticket into a slot on the front of the machine. Either action will open the gates for valid tickets to let the passenger through. As can be seen here, such barriers have to be staffed. This is **Stratford** on 14 April 2008.

Left: The station at **Kensington Olympia** dates from 2 June 1862, but has been through many trials and tribulations. It was first served by the Metropolitan Railway in a service from the north via Latimer Road, but this came to an abrupt end following bombing on 19 October 1940 and was never resumed. Post-war saw services provided by the District Line from 20 December 1946, but this was operated only when there was an exhibition at the nearby Olympia site. At its lowest ebb in the 1960s, only the District service ran, together with a Monday-to-Fridays workers' service from Clapham Junction. This operated twice outward in the morning and twice back in the afternoon. For a time, InterCity trains called there. Today, the station is operated by London Overground. It has a regular daily Underground service to Earl's Court and terminating at High Street Kensington, plus services to Clapham Junction, Willesden Junction and Watford Junction. That includes operations by Southern. This is a view of the west side station entrance on 4 August 2003.

Centre left: For many years, **Kensington Olympia** was known as Kensington Addison Road; a new sign on the east side of the line now directs passengers to the station and is seen here on 4 August 2003.

Below left: The District Line service uses what is now a single line stub to Platform 1 (right) at **Kensington Olympia**, where it shares with northbound National Rail services on Platform 2. A glazed canopy is provided for passenger use in this view of 4 August 2003.

Above right: **Southfields** is the station for the Wimbledon tennis fortnight, and some form of platform decoration is usually managed. This is the scene during Wimbledon 2000. A shuttle bus service to the Courts is provided from outside the station.

Right: The Piccadilly Line station at **Hounslow East** has been totally reconstructed, and work on the westbound side is almost complete in this view of 22 March 2003. In best Underground tradition, a very distinctive design has been employed. How different from the 'station kit' approach of Network Rail where, to keep costs to a minimum, the modular building approach is again in vogue.

Left: **Bank** station is, of course, associated with the Bank of England and the City of London in general. This motif of the City's Gryphons, pictured on 29 March 2008, has appeared on some of the Underground platforms as part of their refurbishment. The City is the oldest local authority in England, going back at least to the year 1032 and probably much further.

Below left: The platforms of the Waterloo & City Line at **Waterloo** lie directly beneath the main-line station. The primary purpose of this line is, and always has been, to get rail passengers who wanted the City to their destination as expediently as possible. That it was taken over by London Underground in 1994 was more to do with keeping it out of the problems of privatisation than its attractiveness to LU. This is the departure platform at Waterloo on Saturday 29 March 2008, showing the newly acquired hump in the platform to allow level boarding. It would never be so empty at 08.41 during the week.

Above right: The station at **Wembley Park** was opened for regular public use on 12 May 1894, and has since been rebuilt, in 1923, for the British Empire Exhibition; and in 2005 for the new Wembley Stadium. This view of 9 April 2008 shows the new and capacious staircase leading down from the ticket hall area to pass under the A4089 and into Olympic Way. Its mere size is an indication of the importance of such traffic and the effort needed to be put in to cater for it successfully.

Below: **Wembley Park** station has been extended substantially, and this new design of seating has been installed extensively over the Underground system. In a survey of 1993, London Underground counted more than 80 different styles of bench seating, both original and modern. The aim then was to restore the old ones wherever possible and limit the modern ones to three basic and related designs. It is 9 April 2008.

Left: **Kensal Green** station opened on 1 October 1916 for use by Bakerloo Line trains; the main-line services came later, in 1922. The recently rebuilt station entrance and ticket office at street level clearly owe little to 55 Broadway, and it was indeed a National Rail station until November 2007 when it became a London Underground station. It is 7 May 2008.

Centre left: The platforms at **Kensal Green** are reached by covered stairways; both platforms boast extensive canopy cover. In this view of 7 May 2008, looking a little south of west (for the nominally northbound direction), are the 290m Kensal Green tunnels on the so-called 'dc electric lines'. Services are provided by London Overground between London Euston and Watford Junction but also by those Bakerloo trains which continue beyond Queens Park to Harrow & Wealdstone. London Underground ownership is confirmed by the roundels bearing the station name.

Below left: Today, **Willesden Junction** is a two-level station catering for the North London Line at high level and for the Bakerloo and London Overground Lines at low level and as seen here in this 7 May 2008 general view. This part opened on 15 June 1912; there have been no platforms on the main line since 1962. The station has changed little in recent years, other than the new exit and ticket office arrangements which can be seen to the right. This station is now operated by London Overground.

Above right: **Harrow & Wealdstone** station was opened on 20 July 1837 by the London & North Western Railway and was reached by Bakerloo Line trains on 16 April 1917 (though they were withdrawn between September 1982 and June 1984). These use the westernmost platforms nos 1 & 2, and shown here on 7 May 2008 is the direct but subsidiary exit for those arriving from the south. Such passengers thus use the Harrow (as opposed to the Wealdstone) side of the station. The station operator is now London Underground.

Right: Underground trains have not run north of **Harrow & Wealdstone** since 1982, other than to a reversing siding between the running lines. In this view of 7 May 2008, a London Overground train consisting of a Class 313 unit can be seen in the distance proceeding towards Watford Junction. The overbridge connects to the other platforms as well as the station building and exit on the east side of the station.

Left: This sculpture is entitled 'The Time Terminus'. It stands outside **Leytonstone** station, close to the west side entrance, and was photographed on 16 May 2003. It was designed by Lodewyk Pretor in 1999 as the focal point of the then new local transport interchange. It consists of a circular brick-built seat, above which is mounted a sculpture of double and single-deck buses, a tramcar, and other motorised public transport vehicles of various ages.

BIBLIOGRAPHY

abc London Underground Stations, David Leboff, Ian Allan Publishing 1994.
London Underground Stations, A Social and Architectural Study, Laurence Menear, Midas Books 1983.
Charles Holden, Architect. Eitan Carol, Shaun Tyas 2007.
Great Eastern Journal (Great Eastern Railway Society), various issues.
A History of London Transport. T. C. Barker and Michael Robbins, George Allen & Unwin, vol 1 1963, vol 2 1974.
London's Metropolitan Railway. Alan A. Jackson, David & Charles 1986.
Railway Passenger Stations in England, Scotland and Wales: A Chronology. M. E. Quick, 3rd edition, Railway & Canal Historical Society 2005.
The Man Who Built London Transport (A Biography of Frank Pick). Christian Barman, David & Charles 1979.
Underground Architecture. David Lawrence, Capital Transport Publishing 1994.
Series of books on individual Underground lines, Capital Transport Publishing, various authors and dates.